God's
DAILY
ANSWER

devotions to renew your soul

for Mothers

Manuscript written by Vicki J. Kuyper in conjunction with Snapdragon Editorial Group, Inc., Tulsa, Oklahoma.

Cover Design by Denise Rosser
Page Layout by Bart Dawson

ISBN: 1-4041-8478-3

Printed in the United States of America

God's DAILY ANSWER

---

devotions to renew your soul

---

for Mothers

God is inscrutable—there will always be aspects of His person we aren't capable of understanding. But He knows our need for answers and has responded by giving us the Scriptures, rich oral traditions, and the witness of our hearts to let us know what we can expect from Him, how He wishes to interact with us, and the various aspects of His character. He encourages us to ask, seek, and find.

If you are a mother, wondering about what God expects of you, God's Daily Answer for Mothers was designed for you. As you read, you will hear what God has to say about the issues you are facing as you raise your children—topics like balance, faith, patience, protection, and the future. We hope you will also come to know more intimately the One who holds all the answers—the One who holds you in the palm of His hand.

Table of Contents

When God thought of mother,
he must have laughed with satisfaction
and framed it quickly—so rich, so deep,
so divine, so full of soul, power,
and beauty was the conception.

HENRY WARD BEECHER

Fresh Start

God, make a fresh start in me,
shape a Genesis week from the chaos of my life.

PSALM 51:10 THE MESSAGE

*M*otherhood can be a wild ride. From birth to adolescence and beyond, every day is an adventure. You may wish that some moments would never end, while others may be far from what you'd like recorded in the baby book.

But one of God's priceless gifts to you is a fresh start. The mother you were last year, last week, or even just a moment ago is not the parent you're destined to be tomorrow. God is guiding you—just like He is guiding your children—toward growth and change.

Leave yesterday behind. Grab hold of your second chance—or your hundredth—and with God's help, dare to become the mother He created you to be.

If you have made mistakes, even serious ones,
there is always another chance for you.
What we call failure is not the falling down,
but the staying down.

MARY PICKFORD

I like sunrises, Mondays, and new seasons.
God seems to be saying,
"With me you can always start afresh."

ADA LUM

Each day is a new life. Seize it. Live it.

DAVID GUY POWERS

With each sunrise, we start anew.

AUTHOR UNKNOWN

You have begun to live the new life,
in which you are being made new
and are becoming like the One who made you.

COLOSSIANS 3:10 NCV

Kindness

The younger women must be sensible and kind.

TITUS 2:5 CEV

*K*indness doesn't announce its entrance with noisy fanfare. It isn't motivated by mood and doesn't demand center stage. On the contrary, it often works in the shadows—quietly, patiently, consistently—only revealing itself through the gentle whisper of a helping hand or an uplifting word.

Being kind to your children when others are watching, and more importantly when they are not, takes strong intent and the power of God working through your life.

Today, look for opportunities to nurture your own kind heart toward even greater maturity. Ask God to help you reflect His own character by modeling kindness in an often-unkind world.

Be the living expression of God's kindness:
kindness in your face, kindness in your eyes,
kindness in your smile,
kindness in your warm greeting.

MOTHER TERESA

Constant kindness can accomplish much.
As the sun makes ice melt, kindness causes
misunderstanding, mistrust and hostility
to evaporate.

ALBERT SCHWEITZER

A kind heart is a fountain of gladness,
making everything in its vicinity
freshen into smiles.

WASHINGTON IRVING

Be kind. Remember that everyone you meet
is fighting a hard battle.

HARRY THOMPSON

As God's chosen people, holy and dearly loved,
clothe yourselves with compassion, kindness,
humility, gentleness and patience.

COLOSSIANS 3:12 NIV

Thankfulness

Thank God for his Son—
a gift too wonderful for words!

2 CORINTHIANS 9:15 NLT

*Y*ou cook. You clean. You carpool. You read bedtime stories and kiss bruised knees. Your love, your gifts, and your hard work are worthy of gratitude. Words of thanks don't always roll off of toddlers' tongues or into adolescents' daily conversation. But when they do, they warm a mother's heart.

Why not take a moment to warm the heart of your heavenly Father? Just like you, He gives to His children out of love, not a need for gratitude. However, hearing a simple "thank you" touches His heart the same way it touches yours.

Right now, recall how God has cared for you and your family just since you awakened this morning. Let your gratitude grow until it overflows into sincere words of thanks.

Thou has given so much to me.
Give me one thing more—a grateful heart.

GEORGE HERBERT

Thanksgiving is the end of all human conduct,
whether observed in words or works.

J. B. LIGHTFOOT

No duty is more urgent than
that of returning thanks.

SAINT AMBROSE

Thanksgiving is good but thanks-living is better.

MATTHEW HENRY

No matter what happens, always be thankful.

1 THESSALONIANS 5:18 NLT

*Our lives get in step with God and all others
by letting him set the pace.*

ROMANS 3:27 THE MESSAGE

To achieve proper balance, a tightrope walker needs to find just the right pace at which to move forward. A mother's life is a similar balancing act. Trying to fit too many activities and expectations into a single day, or season of life, transforms every hour into rush hour. When this happens, it's easy to lose your balance altogether, causing your emotions, family life, and spiritual growth to take a tumble.

God wants to guide you on a steady path at a healthy pace. That pace may change with time. Being sensitive to what God wants you to do and learning to say no are the first steps toward leading a balanced life. Ask for God's wisdom as you review today's "to do" list.

Raising children is not unlike a long-distance race in which the contestants must learn to pace themselves. ... That is the secret of winning.

JAMES C. DOBSON

Children just don't fit into a "to do" list
very well. It takes time to be an effective parent.

JAMES C. DOBSON

"Holy leisure" refers to a sense of balance in
the life, an ability to be at peace through
the activities of the day, an ability to rest
and take time to enjoy beauty,
an ability to pace ourselves.

RICHARD J. FOSTER

Prescription for a happier and healthier life:
resolve to slow your pace; learn to say no
gracefully; resist the temptation
to chase after more pleasures, hobbies,
and more social entanglements.

JAMES C. DOBSON

Oh, that my steps might be steady,
keeping to the course you set.

PSALM 119:5 THE MESSAGE

Comfort

This is what the LORD says: " ... As a mother comforts her child, so will I comfort you."

ISAIAH 66:12–13 NIV

No matter how old you are, there is a parent whose arms are always open, waiting to hold you close to His heart, a Father who longs to dry your tears with His loving words and provide hope and healing. God is there, no matter how dark the day or deep the wound.

When you're hurting, take a lesson from your children. Run with total abandon to the parent who'll never withhold His love and care for you. Don't hold back. Tell God how you feel. Cry your eyes dry. Read a few psalms. Then, sit quietly, knowing He is near. Ask your Father for comfort. Then, watch for the creative ways in which He answers your heartfelt prayer.

No affliction nor temptation, no guilt nor power of sin, no wounded spirit nor terrified conscience should induce us to despair of help and comfort from God!

THOMAS SCOTT

In Christ the heart of the Father is revealed.
The higher comfort there cannot be than
to rest in the Father's heart.

ANDREW MURRAY

It will greatly comfort you if you can see
God's hand in both your losses and your crosses.

CHARLES HADDON SPURGEON

God does not comfort us to make us
comfortable, but to make us comforters.

ABRAHAM LINCOLN

Whenever I am anxious and worried,
you comfort me and make me glad.

PSALM 94:19 GNT

Humility

Jesus said, "Those who exalt themselves
will be humbled, and those who
humble themselves will be exalted."

MATTHEW 23:12 NLT

A humble mom has a relationship-building vocabulary. "Thank you," "I'm sorry," and "I forgive you" come easily to her lips. She freely acknowledges the part others, including God, play in her success. She doesn't refer to her own weaknesses in negative terms, but instead recognizes how her heavenly Father is refining her character as time goes by.

Pride is a roadblock in this maturing process. What part does it play in your life?

Does it crop up in relation to your talents and abilities, your children's accomplishments, your physical appearance, the décor of your home? There's nothing wrong with taking pride in a job well done. Just remember God's part in the process. Worship Him, instead of the praise of others.

Humility is nothing else but a true knowledge
and awareness of oneself as one really is.

THE CLOUD OF UNKNOWING

It is no great thing to be humble when
you are brought low; but to be humble when
you are praised is a great and rare attainment.

BERNARD OF CLAIRVAUX

For those who would learn God's ways,
humility is the first thing, humility is the second,
humility is the third.

SAINT AUGUSTINE OF HIPPO

If you are humble, nothing will touch you,
neither praise nor disgrace,
because you know what you are.

MOTHER TERESA

Humble yourselves before the Lord,
and he will lift you up.

JAMES 4:10 NIV

Friendship

*These God-chosen lives all around—
what splendid friends they make!*
PSALM 16:3 THE MESSAGE

Your life is surrounded by people. Some of them you've known for years. Others, you have yet to meet. Even though God has placed these people in your life, you may still feel alone, unaware of the relational bounty that surrounds you, the friendships waiting to be developed.

God longs to bless you through others. However, enjoying vibrant friendships takes effort on your part. So, make a phone call. Write a letter. Send an e-mail. Or just gather up the courage to ask, "What's new with you?"

Don't let the demands of motherhood tempt you to put other relationships on hold. You need a helping hand and a listening ear more than ever. Learning to love others, and accepting their love, will help you be a more loving and fulfilled mom.

Friendship is one of the sweetest joys of life.
Many might have failed beneath the bitterness
of their trial had they not found a friend.
CHARLES HADDON SPURGEON

A true friend unbosoms freely, advises justly,
assists readily, adventures boldly,
takes all patiently, defends courageously,
and continues a friend unchangeably.

WILLIAM PENN

Friendship doesn't make you wealthy, but
true friendship will reveal the wealth within you.

AUTHOR UNKNOWN

Friendship is the inexpressible comfort of
feeling safe with a person, having neither
to weigh thoughts nor measure words.

GEORGE ELIOT

*Jesus said, "Greater love has no one than this,
than to lay down one's life for his friends."*

JOHN 15:13

Grace

The Lord said to me, "My grace is sufficient for you, for My strength is made perfect in weakness."

2 Corinthians 12:9

God sees you differently than most people do. That's because He looks at you through a veil of grace. He knows you better than you know yourself. He's aware of both the good and bad choices you've made in life. Yet, because of Jesus' sacrifice, He looks at you as clean, whole, and worthy of His unending love.

Picture how you look at your own children. You give a toddler the grace to spill her milk, because you know her limitations—you love her anyway. Your gift of grace gives your child the courage to risk trying again.

With God, you can risk both success and failure. You can move forward with confidence. God's grace will never fail, even when you fall.

There is nothing but God's grace. We walk upon it; we breathe it; we live and die by it; it makes the nails and axles of the universe.

Robert Louis Stevenson

Grace is always given to those ready
to give thanks for it.

THOMAS À KEMPIS

Grace is love that cares and stoops and rescues.

JOHN STOTT

A state of mind that sees God in everything is
evidence of growth in grace and a thankful heart.

CHARLES FINNEY

You have been saved by grace because you believe.
You did not save yourselves. It was a gift from God.

EPHESIANS 2:8 ICB

The glory of GOD—let it last forever!
Let GOD enjoy his creation!

PSALM 104:31 THE MESSAGE

*P*lay has a purpose. It stretches your mind and awakens your creativity. When enjoyed with others, it encourages relationship, laughter, and relaxation. Play is good for kids and grown-ups alike.

It's even good for God. The Bible says that what God created gave Him pleasure. God could have regarded making the earth just one more thing on His eternal "to do" list. Yet, He took the time and effort to creatively fashion whales and warthogs, apple trees and aspens, you and your children. Each creation is unique, a masterpiece whose intricacy and originality is beyond human comprehension. And God had fun making it.

Follow God's example by taking some time today to simply play with your kids, regardless of their age—or yours.

A person who is to be happy must
actively enjoy his blessings.

CICERO

I asked God for all things so I could enjoy life.
He gave me life so I could enjoy all things.

AUTHOR UNKNOWN

In commanding us to glorify him,
God is iviting us to enjoy him.

C. S. LEWIS

Work and play are an artificial pair of opposites
because the best kind of play contains an element
of work, and the most productive kind of work
must include something of the spirit of play.

SYDNEY J. HARRIS

You worked hard and deserve all you've got coming.
Enjoy the blessing! Revel in the goodness!

PSALM 128:2 THE MESSAGE

Benevolence

The Master said … "Turn both your pockets and your heart inside out and give generously to the poor."
LUKE 11:41 THE MESSAGE

There is someone in this world who desperately needs what you can give. The size of the gift isn't important. But the size of the heart behind it can transform a simple donation into a life-changing blessing—for the one who gives, as well as the one who receives.

Ask God to help open your eyes to the needs of those in your community, as well as around the world. The more you can put yourself in another mother's shoes—one who cannot meet her own children's needs—the more God can teach you how to love others in a practical way, by sharing the gifts He's so generously given you.

You are never more like God than when you give.
CHARLES R. SWINDOLL

Feel for others—in your pocket.

CHARLES HADDON SPURGEON

The true source of cheerfulness is benevolence.
The soul that perpetually overflows with
kindness and sympathy will always be cheerful.

PARKE GODWIN

Giving is the secret of a healthy life.
Not necessarily money, but whatever a man has of
encouragement and sympathy and understanding.

JOHN D. ROCKEFELLER JR.

Jesus said, "It is more blessed to give than to receive."

ACTS 20:35

The LORD will guide you always.

ISAIAH 58:11 NIV

magine taking your kids on a guided tour of a natural history museum. How would you feel if you found out your tour guide was not only invisible, but that his voice was almost inaudible? Your first thought might be, Some great guide this is!

That's how some people feel about God's guidance. But God doesn't want you to wander around aimlessly. He promises to point the way—through the Scriptures, prayer, and the advice of others who know Him well.

When you're faced with a big decision, remember you have a Guide who never leaves your side. Pray for wisdom. See what the Bible has to say about your choices. Ask godly friends for input. Then, take what you know and act on it.

Deep in your heart it is not guidance that you want as much as a guide.

JOHN WHITE

I know not the way God leads me,
but well do I know my Guide.

MARTIN LUTHER

The teacher of teachers gives his guidance
noiselessly. I have never heard him speak,
and yet I know that he is within me.
At every moment he instructs me and guides me.
And whenever I am in need of it,
he enlightens me afresh.

THERESE OF LISIEUX

When we fail to wait prayerfully for
God's guidance and strength, we are saying
with our actions, if not our lips,
that we do not need him.

CHARLES HUMMEL

Lord, tell me your ways. Show me how to live.
Guide me in your truth.

PSALM 25:4–5 ICB

Church

They joined with the other believers in
regular attendance at the apostles' teaching sessions
and at the Communion services and prayer meetings.

Acts 2:39 TLB

*Y*our family is much larger than the number of chairs around your dinner table. Once you chose to follow God, you became part of a family of believers. Getting involved in a local church helps you connect with just a few of the members of God's family. Some of them may feel like old friends the moment you meet them. Others may drive you nuts. But that's all part of learning to love, work, and worship together in an imperfect, human community.

The church is one way God makes His truth visible to the world. What part will you, and your children, play in that picture?

The church is not wood and stone, but
the company of people who believe in Christ.

Martin Luther

The true Church is a living organism, a body,
and believers are joined to it by
the quiet working of the Holy Spirit.

CORNELIUS STAM

We must cease to think of the church as
a gathering of institutions and organizations,
and we must get back the notion that
we are the people of God.

M. LLOYD-JONES

The church is an organism, not an organization;
a movement, not a monument.

CHARLES COLSON

You should not stay away from the church meetings,
as some are doing. But you should meet together
and encourage each other.

HEBREWS 10:25 ICB

*Whoever loves wealth is never satisfied
with his income.*

ECCLESIASTES 5:10 NIV

Whether you work solely at home or also in the marketplace, raising a family while balancing a budget takes planning. If making ends meet seems to get harder every month, don't automatically adjust your bottom line. Readjust your attitude.

Let God help uncover any areas in your life where your love of money, or what it can buy, is tying you up in financial knots. Be brutally honest about yourself and your spending habits. Does purchasing anything, from groceries to a pair of funky pumps, fill a need in you that was designed to be filled by God alone? Ask God for the wisdom and self-control you need to turn to Him, instead of the mall, when your heart is running on empty.

If a person gets his attitude toward money straight, it will help straighten out almost every other area in his life.

BILLY GRAHAM

There is no portion of money that is our money,
and the rest God's money. It is all his;
he made it all, gives it all, and he has
simply trusted it to us for his service.
A servant has two purses, the master's
and his own, but we have only one.

ADOLPHE MONOD

Money has never yet made anyone rich.

SENECA

Use everything as if it belongs to God. It does.
You are his steward.

AUTHOR UNKNOWN

Don't fall in love with money.
Be satisfied with what you have.

HEBREWS 13:5 CEV

Honesty

God-loyal people, living honest lives,
make it much easier for their children.

PROVERBS 20:7 THE MESSAGE

*W*ant to make your kids' lives easier? Tell the truth. Not only to them, but to those around you. Don't invent excuses to turn down unwanted invitations, fudge on your taxes, or lie about your kids' ages to save money at the movies. Tell the truth, the whole truth, and nothing but the truth.

That's what God does with you. He doesn't promise one thing, then deliver another. That's why you can trust what He says—every word, every time.

Give your children that same privilege. Your honesty when they're small will reassure them during the teen years that you're a mom of your word. Your example will also help them see that faith is not just something you believe, but something you live.

If we be honest with ourselves,
we shall be honest with each other.

GEORGE MACDONALD

Honesty has a beautiful and refreshing
simplicity about it. No ulterior motives.
No hidden meanings.

CHARLES R. SWINDOLL

I consider the most enviable of all titles,
the character of an honest man.

GEORGE WASHINGTON

Honesty is the first chapter
in the book of wisdom.

THOMAS JEFFERSON

An honest answer is as pleasing as a kiss on the lips.
PROVERBS 24:26 ICB

Wisdom

Whoever walks with the wise becomes wise.

PROVERBS 13:20 NRSV

*T*he people you hang out with influence the way you think. This group not only includes your spouse and your friends, but those folks you "visit" via talk show, fashion magazine, chat room, or romance novel.

If you long to grow in wisdom, it makes sense to spend quality time with those you can honestly look up to, those whose wisdom is evident through their words, lifestyle, and relationships.

God should be at the top of that list. Spend time getting better acquainted with His words and ways by reading the Bible each day—even a few minutes can have a big impact. Talk to Him in prayer. Turn to Him for answers. Grow wise as you grow closer to the Source of wisdom itself.

The next best thing to being wise oneself
is to live in a circle of those who are.

C. S. LEWIS

Wisdom is the application of knowledge.

AUTHOR UNKNOWN

Wisdom is concerned with how we relate
to people, to the world, and to God.

EDMUND P. CLOWNEY

Wisdom is a gift direct from God.

BOB JONES

If any of you is lacking in wisdom, ask God,
who gives to all generously and ungrudgingly,
and it will be given you.

JAMES 1:5 NRSV

Expectations

My soul, wait silently for God alone,
for my expectation is from Him.

PSALM 62:5

Expectations can keep you going on tough days. The expectation of an upcoming vacation or a visit with a friend can lighten your heart as you plow through a mountain of laundry or overflowing in box. But what happens to your heart when your expectations aren't met? When budget concerns cancel a vacation? When illness postpones a much-anticipated visit? When your kids' actions fall well below your expectations?

Disappointment and resentment are often the result of unmet expectations. That doesn't mean you should go through life without expectations. However, instead of holding them tightly in your heart, put them safely in God's hands. He's the One who's ultimately in control. God can use the unexpected in wonderful ways, fostering new growth and unforeseen blessing.

High expectations are the key to everything.

SAM WALTON

We block Christ's advance in our lives
by failure of expectation.

WILLIAM TEMPLE

There is something new every day
if you look for it.

HANNAH HURNARD

The quality of our expectations determines
the quality of our action.

ANDRÉ GODIN

In the morning, O LORD, you hear my voice;
in the morning I lay my requests before you
and wait in expectation.

PSALM 5:3 NIV

Prayer

*Get down on your knees before the Master;
it's the only way you'll get on your feet.*

JAMES 4:10 THE MESSAGE

Cleaning a toilet bowl ... picking up toys ... drying a toddler's tears ... moms spend a lot of time on their knees. However, it's easy to put off kneeling before a God who doesn't demand your immediate attention. Instead, He waits for you to respond to His patient love.

Prayer is a choice to move toward God through communication. It doesn't matter where or how it's done. Your heart can be on its knees while your body is driving a van filled with kids.

Scheduling quiet times of focused prayer is invaluable. But don't let those longer visits with God take the place of moment-to-moment chats. One word, a simple request, a phrase of thanks or praise all hold power and purpose when shared with your Creator.

Prayer should be the key of the day
and the lock of the night.

THOMAS FULLER

We should speak to God from our own hearts
and talk to him as a child talks to his father.

CHARLES HADDON SPURGEON

All who call on God in true faith, earnestly
from the heart, will certainly be heard, and
will receive what they have asked and desired.

MARTIN LUTHER

Prayer changes things? No! Prayer changes people
and people change things.

PAUL TOURNIER

God listens to us every time we ask him.
So we know that he gives us the things
that we ask from him.

1 JOHN 5:15 NCV

Influence

Follow God's example in everything you do,
because you are his dear children.

EPHESIANS 5:1 NLT

*K*ids imitate their parents. That's how they first learn to walk, to talk, and even to relate to God. Think of your life with your children as being a class that's always in session. Your example sets the stage for those in your care. Like any dedicated teacher, it's helpful to quiz yourself periodically by asking, "Is what I'm doing speaking more loudly than what I'm saying? What lessons am I really teaching?"

The impact of your influence on your children's lives is beyond measure. You can make the most of that influence by imitating the loving ways of your own perfect Parent, your Father in heaven. As His ways transform your ways, your example will have an increasingly positive influence on those around you, both big and small.

It is the most natural thing to be like
the person you live with most,
therefore live most with Jesus Christ.

OSWALD CHAMBERS

The entire ocean is affected by a pebble.

BLAISE PASCAL

Whom you would change, you must first love.

MARTIN LUTHER KING JR.

Children will invariably talk, eat, walk, think,
respond, and act like their parents. ...
Give them a pattern that they can see clearly,
and you give them something that
gold and silver cannot buy.

BILLY GRAHAM

*We can be mirrors that brightly reflect the glory
of the Lord. And as the Spirit of the Lord works
within us, we become more and more like him.*

2 CORINTHIANS 3:18 TLB

Health

The Lord cares about our bodies.

1 Corinthians 6:13 NLT

*Y*ou know the rules ... get adequate sleep, exercise regularly, drink plenty of water, and eat a balanced diet. You can be wise about living a healthy lifestyle, but ultimately your health is more in God's hands than it is in yours.

A well-functioning body is a priceless gift that's easily taken for granted. Use it as a touchstone for prayer. Just the fact that you can breathe, see, and walk is a miracle. Get in the habit of regularly thanking God for His marvelous workmanship.

When anyone in your family struggles with health concerns, remember they are God's concerns as well. Prayer is as important as professional medical care. Don't suffer in silence. The Great Physician makes house calls twenty-four hours a day.

Take care of your health,
that it may serve you to serve God.

Saint Francis de Sales

Look at your health; and if you have it,
praise God and value it next to
a good conscience.

IZAAK WALTON

The one who has health has hope,
and the one who has hope has everything.

ARAB PROVERB

Our prayers should be for a sound mind
in a healthy body.

JUVENAL

*I pray that you may prosper in all things
and be in health, just as your soul prospers.*

3 JOHN 2

Discipline

Those who spare the rod hate their children, but those who love them are diligent to discipline them.

PROVERBS 13:24 NRSV

Administering consistent, loving discipline is hard work. Just ask God. He has more kids than can be counted, and many of them are slow learners, always getting into trouble. Yet, God patiently corrects them, forgives them, and encourages them to keep moving forward.

You can do the same thing with your kids. All it takes is wisdom, perseverance, creativity, and love—distributed in God-sized portions. Those God-sized portions are only available by tapping into the Source Himself.

God knows your kids inside and out, as well as your own personal weaknesses and strengths. So, don't give up when discipline seems too hard to handle. On your own, it is. Let God help. He's been known to do the impossible.

Better a little chiding than
a great deal of heartbreak.

WILLIAM SHAKESPEARE

Discipline and love are not antithetical;
one is a function of the other.

JAMES C. DOBSON

Most parents learn too late that if they castigate,
they should castigate the fault and not the child;
if you reproach a fault, it can be reformed, but if
you attack a personality, it can only defend itself.

SYDNEY J. HARRIS

Don't panic even during the storms of
adolescence. Better times are ahead.

JAMES C. DOBSON

Don't fail to correct your children;
discipline won't hurt them!

PROVERBS 23:13 TLB

Silence

God said, "Stand silent! Know that I am God!"
PSALM 46:10 TLB

Silence is often lacking in a mother's world—except, perhaps, when all of the kids are in bed and fast asleep. But the Bible notes the benefits of silence. Not the least of these being an increased awareness of God. That's makes silence something worth searching for.

Finding a quiet place in a chaotic world doesn't just happen on it's own, however. You need to do your best to welcome it in. Along with setting times during the day when TV and music are turned off, consciously practice putting a stop to the running commentary that often fills your thoughts. Stop and picture yourself in God's presence—which is exactly where you are. Close your eyes for just a moment. Listen … and know.

Silence is but a rich pause in the music of life.
SAROJINI NAIDU

All in me is silent ... I am immersed
in the silence of God.

CATHERINE DE HAECK DOHERTY

Silence, like a poultice, comes
To heal the blows of sound.

OLIVER WENDELL HOLMES

Lord, teach me to silence my own heart that
I may listen to the gentle movement of
the Holy Spirit within me and sense the depths
which are of God.

ELIJAH DE VIDAS

*There is a time for everything, and a season for
every activity under heaven: ...
a time to be silent and a time to speak.*

ECCLESIASTES 3:1, 7 NIV

God's Forgiveness

If we confess our sins,
He is faithful and just to forgive us.

1 John 1:9

*I*magine your kids doing something you've told them not to. Picture yourself having that "discussion" afterwards where you talk things through, reinforcing the rules, doling out appropriate consequences, and grappling with forgiveness. Imagine how you'd feel if you had that same conversation every single day for the very same offense—for the rest of your life. At some point, your patience—and forgiveness—would probably run dry.

But God's forgiveness never does. Coming to God with a contrite heart always yields the same result—absolute forgiveness. That's because Jesus has already paid for what you've done. Let the high price of God's unfailing forgiveness lead you from gratitude to heartfelt repentance, then on toward leading a more godly life.

There is only one person God cannot forgive: the one who refuses to come to him for forgiveness.

Author Unknown

Forgiveness does not mean the cancellation of
all consequences of wrongdoing. It means
the refusal on God's part to let our guilty past
affect His relationship with us.

AUTHOR UNKNOWN

I think that if God forgives us we must
forgive ourselves.

C. S. LEWIS

The most marvelous ingredient in the forgiveness
of God is that he also forgets—the one thing
a human being can never do.

OSWALD CHAMBERS

You, Lord, are good, and ready to forgive.

PSALM 86:5

Beauty

*Don't be concerned about the outward beauty that
depends on fancy hairstyles, expensive jewelry,
or beautiful clothes. You should be known for
the beauty that comes from within.*

1 PETER 3:3–4 NLT

*S*pending time with God is like having the ultimate makeover. God's gentle hand highlights your best features, while His truth helps trim away any ugly attitudes that may be hidden deep inside. God brings out your natural beauty—the beauty He placed within your heart the day He first created you.

The first impression you make on others often includes their perception of what you look like on the outside, the style of your hair or cut of your clothes. But ultimately, it's who you are that will leave a lasting impression. Let that impression be one that not only attracts others to you as a loving person, but to the beauty of God Himself.

Exuberance is beauty.

WILLIAM BLAKE

Our outward imperfections are a reminder of
God's priorities. He is concerned with character;
not the deception of outward beauty.

ERWIN W. LUTZER

If you are born of God; then in you
God will green; his godhead is your sap;
your beauty is in him.

ANGELUS SILESIUS

There is no cosmetic for beauty like happiness.

MARGUERITE COUNTESS OF BLESSINGTON

Charm is deceptive, and beauty is fleeting;
but a woman who fears the LORD is to be praised.

PROVERBS 31:30 NIV

I will greatly rejoice in the LORD,
my soul shall be joyful in my God.

ISAIAH 61:10

Not everything that happens to you today will inspire joy to bubble up to the surface of your life. However, there is a never-ending Source of joy close at hand. His Spirit is alive in your heart, comforting you when life is hard, encouraging you when friends let you down, strengthening you when your own energy is at an end, and opening your eyes to simple delights that could easily be overlooked.

God's presence and purpose in your life can turn ordinary days—or even really bad, no good, awful days—into opportunities to discover a joy that goes deeper than circumstances and lasts longer than time itself.

Happiness depends on what happens; joy does not.

OSWALD CHAMBERS

Joy is the most infallible sign of the presence of God.

LEON BLOY

Life need not be easy to be joyful.
Joy is not the absence of trouble but
the presence of Christ.

WILLIAM VAN DER HOVEN

Joy is an unceasing fountain bubbling up in the heart; a secret spring the world can't see and doesn't know anything about.

DWIGHT MOODY

*Jesus said, "Ask and you will receive.
And your joy will be the fullest joy."*

JOHN 16:24 ICB

Faithfulness

Never let go of loyalty and faithfulness.

PROVERBS 3:3 GNT

A faithful mom is someone her kids can trust. Her yes doesn't mean "if it happens to be convenient at the time." Her no doesn't imply "unless you wear me down to the point where I no longer care." She says what she means and means what she says—that includes doing everything in her power to keep her promises.

Can your kids, your friends, your spouse, and God trust what you say? If you have trouble following through on commitments, ask God to stop you before you make them. Carefully consider what you're about to say. Is it wholly true? Is it reasonable? Is it right? When you're true to your word, God's own faithful character is more visible through you.

We know that our rewards depend
not on the job itself but on the faithfulness
with which we serve God.

JOHN PAUL I

Faithfulness in little things is a big thing.

SAINT JOHN CHRYSOSTOM

God did not call us to be successful,
but to be faithful.

MOTHER TERESA

He does most in God's great world
who does his best in his own little world.

THOMAS JEFFERSON

The LORD preserves the faithful.

PSALM 31:23 NIV

Priorities

*In everything you do, put God first, and
he will direct you and crown your efforts with success.*

PROVERBS 3:6 TLB

When honoring God is your top priority, your life shows it—but not in the way some people expect. You may not work on the foreign mission field or pray more eloquently than any other mom you know. The truth is, putting God first may look different in your life than it does in the life of anyone else on the planet.

That's because making God number one simply means following His number-one rule: love Him above all and love others as you would yourself. As love guides your decisions, your other priorities will fall into place. Your actions may differ from situation to situation, but your motives will remain steadfast—honoring God with your heart, soul, mind, and strength.

~ ~ ~

When you put God first, you are establishing order
for everything else in your life.

ANDREA GARNEY

God first, others second, self last.

AUTHOR UNKNOWN

When first things are put first,
second things are not suppressed but increased.

C. S. LEWIS

Do not let the good things in life rob you
of the best things.

BUSTER ROTHMAN

Jesus said, "The thing you should want most
is God's kingdom and doing what God wants."

MATTHEW 6:33 NCV

Children

Children are a gift from God; they are his reward.

PSALM 127:3 TLB

Your kids can learn a lot from you. However, you can learn just as much from them. They can teach you lessons, like the wonder of a ladybug, the pleasure of an afternoon nap, and the fun of letting yourself get dirty now and then. They can also teach you about the depth of God's love.

Consider how you feel as a parent when your kids are sad, joyful, courageous, funny, curious, kind, or even in pain. Let your own emotions serve as a touchstone of how God feels about you. Then, go deeper. Remember, God's love is perfect, never tarnished by selfishness, exhaustion, or a busy schedule.

Take a moment right now to bask in the gift of God's love for you.

~ ~ ~

Making the decision to have a child is momentous—it is to decide forever to have your heart go walking around outside your body.

ELIZABETH STONE

A rose can say I love you,
Orchids can enthrall,
But a weed bouquet in a chubby fist,
Oh my, that says it all!

AUTHOR UNKNOWN

Holding a beggar's child
Against my heart,
Through blinding tears I see
That as I love the tiny, piteous thing,
So God loves me!

TOYOHIKO KAGAWA

We never know the love of a parent until
we become parents ourselves.

HENRY WARD BEECHER

He gives children to the woman who has none.
He makes her a happy mother.

PSALM 113:9 ICB

Satisfaction

*Enjoy what you have rather than desiring
what you don't have.*

ECCLESIASTES 6:9 NLT

*B*eing satisfied with what you have, where you are, and who God created you to be is a key to finding happiness. But holding a key isn't the same thing as using it. It's easy to compare your life with those around you—or even with the ads on TV. The more you measure what God's given you against the lives of those you feel God's been even more generous to, the less satisfied you'll feel.

When the itch of dissatisfaction creeps into your heart, try a little "reverse psychology" on yourself. Look at those whose lives are harder than your own. Read the paper. Watch the news. Consider those you're praying for. Open your eyes afresh to the joy of where you are.

Contentment is understanding that if
I am not satisfied with what I have,
I will never be satisfied with what I want.

BILL GOTHARD

Do not give your heart to that which
does not satisfy your heart.

ABBA POEMEN

Fulfillment comes as a by-product of our love
for God. And that satisfaction is better
than we ever imagined.

ERWIN W. LUTZER

The world without Christ will not
satisfy the soul.

THOMAS BROOKS

As for me, I shall behold your face in righteousness;
when I awake I shall be satisfied,
beholding your likeness.

PSALM 17:15 NRSV

Fellowship

If we are living in the light of God's presence,
just as Christ does, then we have wonderful fellowship
and joy with each other.

1 JOHN 1:7 TLB

*F*inding out you have something in common with another mom forms an automatic bond. Maybe both of you play Bunco, your sons love whales, or you both gave birth in Akron—to twins.

When the paths of two people who love God cross, there's a connection that goes far deeper than common interests or coincidence. The awareness that God is at work in both of your lives automatically makes you family.

These kinds of family ties are an important part of God's plan for your life. Praying together, holding each other accountable, and helping dry one another's tears are all ways that God shows His love to you through someone else. Give Him the chance to bless you in that way today.

No person is an island, entire of itself,
every person is a piece of the continent,
a part of the main.

JOHN DONNE

The virtuous soul that is alone and without
a master is like a lone burning coal;
it will grow colder rather than hotter.

JOHN OF THE CROSS

The only basis for real fellowship with God
and man is to live out in the open with both.

ROY HESSION

Be united with other Christians.
A wall with loose bricks is not good.
The bricks must be cemented together.

CORRIE TEN BOOM

Do not be interested only in your own life,
but be interested in the lives of others.

PHILIPPIANS 2:4 ICB

Courage

Stand true to what you believe.
Be courageous. Be strong.

1 CORINTHIANS 16:13 NLT

*S*ometimes, courage sheds a tear. It may even quake in its boots or consider turning back. But one thing courage never does is give up. It moves forward, regardless of what lies ahead, because of this one thing: God has asked the one who bears it to do so.

Is there anything God is asking you to do that you keep putting off or perhaps have run away from altogether? Take courage. God would never let you face what you're afraid of alone. He's there beside you, guiding you, comforting you, making you strong. He wants you to see firsthand that with Him, you can do more than you ever dreamed possible.

Have plenty of courage. God is stronger than the Devil. We are on the wining side.

JOHN WILBUR CHAPMAN

Courage is doing what you're afraid to do.

EDDIE RICKENBACHER

Courage is fear that has said its prayers.

DOROTHY BERNARD

Courage consists, not in blindly
overlooking danger, but
in seeing and conquering it!

JEAN PAUL RICHTER

Be strong and of good courage, do not fear
nor be afraid of them; for the LORD your God,
He is the One who goes with you.

DEUTERONOMY 31:6

Words

What you say can mean life or death.
Those who speak with care will be rewarded.

PROVERBS 18:21 NCV

*E*very day you have the opportunity to give priceless gifts to those around you. They're called "words." They have the power to heal, encourage, teach, and inspire. It is up to you to decide how well the gift fits the one you're giving it to. The more you allow God to work in your heart, to make your thoughts pure and your motives loving, the more beneficial your gifts will be.

Ill-fitting words are thoughtless gifts. Not only are they worthless, but they often cause damage, instead of spreading blessing. Carefully choose the gifts you're going to bestow today. Although you have an unlimited supply, once given to someone, they are nonreturnable.

Kind words produce their image on men's souls,
and a beautiful image it is.
They smooth, and quiet, and comfort the hearer.

BLAISE PASCAL

Good words are worth much and cost little.
SIR GEORGE HERBERT

Speaking without thinking is shooting
without aiming.
SIR WILLIAM GURNEY BENHAM

It is easier to look wise than to talk wisely.
SAINT AMBROSE

When you talk, do not say harmful things.
But say what people need—words that will help others
become stronger.
EPHESIANS 4:29 ICB

Ask where the good way is, and walk in it,
and you will find rest for your souls.

JEREMIAH 6:16 NIV

When your body is weary, everything you do is affected. Your mind isn't quite as quick. Your patience isn't quite as long. Your stamina runs out. The same thing is true of your soul. A weary soul affects your attitudes and actions toward God and those around you.

Give your soul a break. Spend time with the only One in whom your soul can find true rest. Talk to God about your day. Sit quietly, just knowing He's near. Read a psalm or two. Relax with a Christian biography. Count the stars God's made for you to enjoy. Sing your very own song of thanks and praise.

Anytime's the right time to find refreshment with the One you love.

Jesus knows we must come apart and rest a while,
or else we may just plain come apart.

VANCE HAVNER

There is no music in a rest,
but there is the making of music in it.

JOHN RUSKIN

Take rest; a field that has rested
gives a bountiful crop.

OVID

How beautiful it is to do nothing,
and then rest afterward.

SPANISH PROVERB

Jesus said, "Come to me, all you that are weary
and are carrying heavy burdens,
and I will give you rest."

MATTHEW 11:28 NRSV

Acceptance

Honor God by accepting each other,
as Christ has accepted you.

ROMANS 15:7 CEV

*Y*ou're a bundle of strengths and weaknesses, a work in progress. So is everyone you know, including your kids. God accepts each of you exactly where you are. He knows that today you're a step beyond where you were yesterday, but you're still not quite up to who you can become tomorrow.

God's acceptance is grounded in ever-patient love, a love so deep He sent His own Son to die for you, even when you had no regard for Him. How easily does your love reach out and accept those who don't live up to your "standards"? Ask God to help you accept others where they are, while still encouraging them to become all God created them to be.

~ ~ ~

If God accepts me as I am,
then I had better do the same.

HUGH MONTEFIORE

A ccept the fact that you are accepted.

PAUL TILLICH

J esus accepts you the way you are,
but loves you too much to leave you that way.

LEE VENDEN

J ust as I am, thou wilt receive, will welcome,
pardon, cleanse, relieve; because thy promise
I believe, O Lamb of God, I come.

CHARLOTTE ELLIOTT

To the praise of the glory of His grace,
by which He hah made us accepted in the Beloved.

EPHESIANS 1:6

Meditation

Let the words of my mouth and the meditation
of my heart be acceptable in Your sight, O LORD,
my strength and my Redeemer.

PSALM 19:14

*M*editating on those you love comes naturally. When a woman is engaged, she thinks about her fiancé all the time. She ponders his attributes, their future together, and what to do to please him. When you became pregnant, you did much the same thing. You mused about the little person you hadn't yet met, but loved beyond measure.

Though you haven't seen God, the more you love Him, the more you'll meditate on Him. You'll do more than read the Bible. You'll think about what you've read throughout the day. God's words will become precious, like the words of a fiancé to his bride-to-be. You'll contemplate God's actions, dream about the day you'll see Him face-to-face, and let His presence influence every area of your life.

Let us leave the surface and, without leaving the world, plunge into God.

TEILHARD DE CHARDIN

Those who draw water from the wellspring
of meditation know that God dwells
close to their hearts.

TOYOHIKO KAGAWA

In the rush and noise of life, as you have
intervals, step home within yourselves and be still.
Wait upon God, and feel his good presence;
this will carry you evenly through
your day's business.

WILLIAM PENN

Meditation is the activity of calling to mind,
and thinking over, and dwelling on, and applying
to oneself, the various things that one knows
about the works and ways and purposes and
promises of God.

J. I. PACKER

May my meditation be sweet to Him.

PSALM 104:34

Faith

We walk by faith, not by sight.
2 Corinthians 5:7 NRSV

When you were pregnant, you had faith that there was a child growing inside you. The doctor said there was. The fact that your clothes no longer fit confirmed it was true. But you didn't actually meet that child until several months later. Yet, you had faith you were about to become a mother. So you took appropriate action. You set up a nursery, sought proper medical care, and prepared yourself for parenthood.

In the same way, faith in God also takes action. Even though you do not see Him, you believe in Him and that you will one day live with Him in heaven. This should affect how you conduct yourself today. You should act on what you know … that God loves you and those around you. Those who turn to Him will spend eternity in His presence. God's power working through you can show them the way.

Let what you believe make a difference in your life, and the world, today.

The act of faith is more than a bare statement of belief; it is a turning to the face of the living God.
Christopher Bryant

Faith is nothing at all tangible.
It is simply believing God.

HANNAH WHITALL SMITH

Faith is to believe what you do not yet see:
the reward for this faith is to see
what you believe.

SAINT AUGUSTINE OF HIPPO

Faith tells us of things we have never seen
and cannot come to know
by our natural senses.

SAINT JOHN OF THE CROSS

Faith is the substance of things hoped for,
the evidence of things not seen.

HEBREWS 11:1

Forgiveness

*Jesus said, "Forgive us the wrongs we have done,
as we forgive the wrongs that others have done to us."*
MATTHEW 6:12 GNT

If your child talks to you over and over again about how afraid she is of dogs, you can be sure of one thing—this topic is of vital importance to her heart.

In the Bible, God talks a lot about forgiveness. Obviously, this topic is important to His heart. Anything that is important to God's heart should be to yours as well. After all, your entire eternity is based on the acceptance of this priceless gift.

Perhaps another reason why God speaks so frequently about forgiveness is because you're going to have so many opportunities to use it. Living with imperfect people guarantees it. Ask God to bring to mind anyone you need to extend this gift to today—including yourself.

Forgiveness is God's command.
MARTIN LUTHER

Forgiveness means letting go of the past.

GERALD JAMPOLSKY

To forgive is to set a prisoner free
and discover the prisoner was you.

AUTHOR UNKNOWN

Forgiveness is the key that unlocks the door of
resentment and the handcuffs of hate.
It is a power that breaks the chains of
bitterness and the shackles of selfishness.

CORRIE TEN BOOM

Be gentle and ready to forgive; never hold grudges.
Remember, the Lord forgave you,
so you must forgive others.

COLOSSIANS 3:13 TLB

Nature

Take a good look at God's wonders—
they'll take your breath away.

PSALM 66:5 THE MESSAGE

*T*ake a walk. Look up at the sky. Whether it's a brilliant blue or filled with dark clouds, there's a majesty about it that can't be denied. Glance at the trees. Inspect the velvet petals of a wildflower. Stroke the dappled fur of a kitten. You're surrounded by miracles, tiny glimpses of God's majesty that have rubbed off of His hands onto all He has made.

Take a moment to thank God for how His creativity fills your heart with joy. Wonder at the complexity of the variety of life God has fashioned, including the individuality of your own children. Just sit in awe of the One who created you—and let praise flow freely from your lips like ocean waves flow toward the shore.

I love to think of nature as an unlimited broadcasting station through which God speaks to us every hour, if we will only tune in.

GEORGE WASHINGTON CARVER

We can almost smell the aroma of God's beauty
in the fresh spring flowers. His breath surrounds us
in the warm summer breezes.

GALE HEIDE

Nature is but a name for an effect
whose cause is God.

WILLIAM COWPER

The more I study nature,
the more I am amazed at the Creator.

LOUIS PASTEUR

The heavens declare the glory of God;
and the firmament shows his handiwork.

PSALM 19:1

Hospitality

*Cheerfully share your home with those who need
a meal or a place to stay.*

*H*ospitality is not just for those with a flair for entertaining. It's for everyone who has something to share, no matter how small. Being hospitable can be as simple as sharing your lunch with a family who's forgotten to bring theirs to a sporting event. It doesn't require a picture-perfect home or a culinary degree.

Being hospitable simply means making others feel at home. If you're like most moms, "home" doesn't resemble a five-star hotel. Don't pressure yourself into pretending it does.

Be real. Be generous. Be empathetic. Use the gifts God's given you in a way that honors others. All you need to do is open your heart every time you open your door. God will help you take it from there.

When there is room in the heart
there is room in the house.

DANISH PROVERB

Hospitality is threefold: for one's family,
this of necessity; for strangers, this of courtesy;
for the poor, this is charity.

THOMAS FULLER

Hospitality is one form of worship.

JEWISH PROVERB

Who practices hospitality entertains
God himself.

AUTHOR UNKNOWN

Share with God's people who are in need.
Practice hospitality.

ROMANS 12:13 NIV

Christ Himself is our peace.

EPHESIANS 2:14 NCV

There is a place of peace on earth. You won't find it in the pages of the morning news. It isn't found in a good book while the kids are taking a nap or even while you're relaxing on a foreign shore during a long-anticipated vacation. It's only found in one place—the presence of God.

When you keep yourself close to God in prayer, even the most chaotic day cannot disturb the peaceful harbor of God's love that surrounds you. That doesn't mean your circumstances, or even your emotions, will always be calm. But putting your trust and hope in God will allow you to face any storm with your head held high and your heart filled with quiet confidence.

Finding God, you have no need to seek peace, for he himself is your peace.

FRANCES J. ROBERTS

If the basis of peace is God, the secret of peace
is trust.

J. N. FIGGIS

Christ alone can bring lasting peace—
peace with God—peace among men
and nations—and peace within our hearts.

BILLY GRAHAM

No God, no peace. Know God, know peace.

AUTHOR UNKNOWN

*You, Lord, give true peace. You give peace
to those who depend on you. You give peace
to those who trust you.*

ISAIAH 26:3 ICB

Family

A wise woman strengthens her family.

PROVERBS 14:1 NCV

amilies are as individual as the people within them. Some have so many common threads it seems nothing could ever pull them apart. Others seem to be a crazy quilt of mismatched pieces. Whatever the makeup of your family, God wants to teach you a lesson in love by letting you live life up close and personal with some people who, like you, are in the process of maturing.

The closer you are to someone, the more likely it is your weaknesses will show. That may not feel comfortable, but it's cause for thanks. It's one way God makes you aware of where you need to grow.

What lessons in love does your family have to teach you today?

A family is a place where principles are hammered and honed on the anvil of everyday living.

CHARLES R. SWINDOLL

The family is an everlasting anchorage,
a quiet harbor.

RICHARD BYRD

Loving relationships are a family's best protection
against the challenges of the world.

BERNIE WIEBE

As the family goes, so goes the nation
and so goes the whole world in which we live.

POPE JOHN PAUL II

It takes wisdom to have a good family,
and it takes understanding to make it strong.

PROVERBS 24:3 NCV

Strength

Be strong in the Lord and in the power of His might.

EPHESIANS 6:10

*D*o you know your own strength? The only way to measure it is to put it to the test. The next time you're faced with troubles that seem too heavy for a heart to bear, obstacles that are too big to go around, or a work load that feels as though it will never let up, discover the strength that is available to you—by recognizing how very weak you are.

Motherhood, and life in general, is not a one-woman job. Only by relying on God's limitless power, will you find the strength to handle the emotional, physical, spiritual, and relational hurdles that come your way.

So, don't be bound by a heavy load you're unable to carry. Lean on God and His boundless strength.

The weaker we feel, the harder we lean on God. And the harder we lean, the stronger we grow.

JONI EARECKSON TADA

The Lord doesn't promise to give us something to
take so we can handle our weary moments.
He promises us himself. That is all.
And that is enough.

CHARLES R. SWINDOLL

They that wait upon the Lord renew
their strength.

LEONARD RAVENHILL

When God is our strength, it is strength indeed;
when our strength is our own, it is only weakness.

SAINT AUGUSTINE OF HIPPO

I can do all things through Christ
because he gives me strength.

PHILIPPIANS 4:13 ICB

God gives us a free gift—
life forever in Christ Jesus our Lord.

ROMANS 6:23 ICB

The perfect gift is one that's chosen by someone who knows you well. It's exactly what you need and comes gratis, no strings attached. God has extended that kind of gift to you. What's even more amazing is the price tag. This is no ordinary trinket, a knickknack that will gather dust. This gift is an open door into eternity.

Though it's free, this gift wasn't cheap. It was paid for in blood. Jesus died on the cross to give you the gift of a lifetime, literally. Your life can no longer be counted in years. What you're experiencing on earth is only the beginning. What awaits is beyond comprehension.

Don't let your gratitude go unspoken. Let your thanks extend as long as your life.

Eternity is not something that begins
after you are dead. It is going on all the time.

CHARLOTTE PERKINS GILMAN

Eternity is the place where questions
and answers become one.

ELI WIESSEL

The life of faith does not earn eternal life;
it is eternal life.

WILLIAM TEMPLE

People who dwell in God dwell
in the Eternal Now.

MEISTER ECKHART

*Jesus said, "Whoever believes in the Son
has eternal life."*

JOHN 3:36 NRSV

Future

Continue to reverence the Lord all the time,
for surely you have a wonderful future ahead of you.

PROVERBS 23:18 TLB

Tomorrow may be a mystery, but your future is a certainty. God has good things planned for you. You have an eternal home, where the Love of your life awaits. Until that day arrives, you have a life to live, filled with countless blessings.

Life here on Earth holds many unexpected twists and turns. But God is right beside you every step of the way. The closer you draw to Him, the more clearly you will be able to see the thread of love that is woven through every single day of your life—and the lives of your children.

Take hold of that thread and follow it all the way Home. Surely, you have a wonderful future ahead of you.

Never be afraid to trust an unknown future
to a known God.

CORRIE TEN BOOM

The only light on the future is faith.

THEODOR HOECKER

The future is God's: which means that,
wherever the individual being goes,
in life or death, God is there.

HANS KÜNG

The future is as bright as the promises of God.

ADONIRAM JUDSON

"I know the plans I have for you," declares the LORD,
"plans to prosper you and not to harm you,
plans to give you hope and a future."

JEREMIAH 29:11 NIV

Worry

*Let petitions and praises shape your worries
into prayers, letting God know your concerns.*
PHILIPPIANS 4:6 THE MESSAGE

God loves you and wants the very best for your life. That's because you're His cherished child. You want the same for your children. That's just the way good parents' hearts are made.

Worrying about your children's happiness, safety, and future may feel natural. But the truth is, worry accomplishes absolutely nothing—except to give you a distracted mind and, perhaps, an upset stomach.

God's antidote to worry is prayer. One by one, place your concerns in the hands of the heavenly Father who loves your children even more than you do. You can trust Him to bring about good in your children's lives, no matter what circumstances they face.

Every evening I turn worries over to God.
He's going to be up all night anyway.
MARY C. CROWLEY

There is nothing so wretched or foolish
as to anticipate misfortunes.
What madness is it in expecting evil
before it arrives.

SENECA

Worry does not empty tomorrow of its sorrow;
it empties today of its strength.

CORRIE TEN BOOM

Worry gives a small thing a big shadow.

SWEDISH PROVERB

*Jesus said, "Which of you by worrying
can add one cubit to his stature?"*

MATTHEW 6:27

Perseverance

*Perseverance must finish its work so that
you may be mature and complete.*

JAMES 1:4 NIV

*I*f you want to see perseverance in action, take a lesson from your kids. Watch how many times a toddler falls, then pulls himself back onto his feet before he masters the art of walking. Consider the work it takes to learn how to read, eat ice cream, or play the piano. Any complex skill takes time to master—including motherhood.

It would be nice if the moment your kids were born, you instinctively knew how to flawlessly guide them to maturity. But while your kids are maturing, so are you. You're each going to take a tumble now and then. When that happens, the only way to move forward is to take hold of God's helping hand, get up, and try again.

Great works are performed, not by strength,
but by perseverance.

SAMUEL JOHNSON

There must be a beginning to any
great matter, but the continuing to the end
until it be thoroughly finished
yields the true glory.

THOMAS CARLYLE

Permanence, perseverance, and persistence
in spite of all obstacles, discouragements,
and impossibilities: It is this, that in all things
distinguishes the strong soul from the weak.

SIR FRANCIS DRAKE

Energy and persistence conquer all things.

BENJAMIN FRANKLIN

*You need to persevere so that when you have done
the will of God, you will receive
what he has promised.*

HEBREWS 10:36 NIV

Success

My protection and success come from God alone.

"*S*uccess" in motherhood is hard to measure. It can't be gauged by your children's grades, athletic abilities, social skills, or smooth transition into adulthood. True success is simply doing your best at the job God has given you to do, regardless of what the results may look like to others.

It's nice to have the accolades of those around you. But they are usually offered only for the victories that are easily seen. Most of the accomplishments of motherhood don't take place on center stage. They happen slowly over time, through encouraging words, consistent prayers, and wise, loving ways.

Turning to God as the definitive child expert, then acting on what you learn, is the only sure road to success for you, and your children.

I have only to be true to the highest I know—
success or failure is in the hands of God.

E. STANLEY JONES

Success is a journey, not a destination.

BEN SWEETLAND

It is not your business to succeed, but to do right;
when you have done so, the rest lies with God.

C. S. LEWIS

He has achieved success who has lived well,
laughed often, and loved much.

BESSIE ANDERSON STANLEY

It is not that we think we can do anything
of lasting value by ourselves.
Our only power and success
come from God.

2 CORINTHIANS 3:5 NLT

Encouragement

Encourage one another daily,
as long as it is called Today.

HEBREWS 3:13 NIV

*E*ncouragement isn't only conveyed through words. It can also be given through a knowing look, a pat on the back, or your tone of voice. Even your presence, silently cheering your son on at a band recital, is encouragement that touches the heart.

Encouraging someone may seem like a small gesture, but the message it conveys is monumental— "I believe in you. You matter to me." Everyone longs to hear those words. Whether that message is spoken audibly or communicated through loving actions, it strengthens the heart of the one it is directed to. It does what the word "encouragement" really means: it imparts courage.

Consider those in your life who could use a dose of courage today. Don't hesitate to offer it.

More people fail for lack of encouragement than for any other reason.

AUTHOR UNKNOWN

If you wish to be disappointed, look to others.
If you wish to be downhearted, look to yourself.
If you wish to be encouraged,
look upon Jesus Christ.

ERICH SAUER

Encouragement is oxygen to the soul.

GEORGE M. ADAMS

Encouragement costs you nothing to give,
but it is priceless to receive.

AUTHOR UNKNOWN

Encourage one another and build each other up,
just as in fact you are doing.

1 THESSALONIANS 5:11 NIV

Identity

Jesus said, "Live out your God-created identity."
MATTHEW 5:48 THE MESSAGE

here's only one you—only one woman, mother, wife, friend, and human being who can offer the world what you can. Yet your identity goes deeper than what you do. It describes who you really are.

The closer you get to God the more you discover your true identity. The core of that identity lies in the fact that you are a child of God, one who is dearly loved and destined to fill a place in the world that no one else was designed to fill.

Be true to that identity. Refuse to be squeezed into a mold that others may feel is more desirable. Trust the design your Creator has chosen. Seek out God's unique plan for your life—then dare to live it.

A vital fringe benefit of being a Christian is the tremendous sense of identity that grows out of knowing Jesus Christ.

JAMES C. DOBSON

When we reject our specialness, water down our
God-given individuality and uniqueness,
we begin to lose our freedom.
The conformist is in no way a free man.

NORMAN VINCENT PEALE

Every man knows well enough that he is
a unique being, only once on this earth;
and by no extraordinary chance will such
a marvelously picturesque piece of diversity in
unity as he is ever be put together a second time.

FRIEDRICH WILHELM NIETZSCHE

Everything is good when it leaves
the Creator's hands.

JEAN-JACQUES ROUSSEAU

Thank you for making me so wonderfully complex!
Your workmanship is marvelous—
and how well I know it.

PSALM 139:14 NLT

Blessings

May the Lord continually bless you with
heaven's blessings as well as with human joys.

PSALM 128:5 TLB

All of God's blessings are good. Some delight your eyes and heart from the very start. Others come concealed in unappealing wrapping paper. It may take awhile to discover the treasure that lies inside. But both kinds of blessings are valuable and worthy of heartfelt thanks.

Look around you. What blessings can you give God thanks for today? The list may include things like your family, your home, your health, food, and finances. Now, consider the unpleasant "gifts" life has brought your way. How is God using them in a positive way? You may not be able to see the answer clearly at this time, but don't stop looking—and offering thanks.

The best things are nearest: breath in your nostrils,
light in your eyes, flowers at your feet, duties
at your hand, the path of God just before you.

ROBERT LOUIS STEVENSON

The more we count the blessings we have,
the less we crave the luxuries we haven't.

WILLIAM ARTHUR WARD

God is more anxious to bestow his blessings
on us than we are to receive them.

SAINT AUGUSTINE OF HIPPO

Reflect upon your present blessings,
of which every man has many,
not on your past misfortunes,
of which all men have some.

CHARLES DICKENS

See if I will not open the windows of heaven
for you and pour down for you
an overflowing blessing.

MALACHI 3:10 NRSV

O LORD, You are our Father;
we are the clay, and You our potter.

ISAIAH 64:8

Change is a part of motherhood, just as it is a part of everyday life. The discipline technique that worked well one day, fails the next. Your hectic schedule is under control, until someone loses his cookies on the seat of the van during the morning commute.

God's plan for life involves change—season to season, minute to minute. The benefit of this plan is that it continually causes you to readjust your focus from your own plans back onto God's.

Being flexible in God's hands means you're willing to go where God leads, at a moment's notice. It means responding with creativity and grace, instead of anger. Pray that when life stretches you to the limit, God will increase your flexibility in wonderful ways.

Better to bend than break.

SCOTTISH PROVERB

We cannot direct the wind,
but we can adjust the sails.

AUTHOR UNKNOWN

Who would be constant in happiness
must often change.

CHINESE PROVERB

God knows what he's about. If he has you
sidelined, out of the action for awhile,
he knows what he's doing. You just stay faithful ...
stay flexible ... stay available ... stay humble,
like David with his sheep.

CHARLES R. SWINDOLL

My times are in Your hand.

PSALM 31:15

Compassion

*Never walk away from someone who deserves help;
your hand is God's hand for that person.*

PROVERBS 3:28 THE MESSAGE

*W*hen your child enters the room in tears, you drop what you're doing and see how you can help. That's because compassion easily springs to the aid of those you love. But how far does your compassion extend? Would it reach out to dry the tears of a stranger? How about comforting a child halfway around the world, someone whose tears you can't see in person, but only hear about secondhand?

God did not give you a compassionate heart just so you could be sympathetic toward the pain of others. He gave it to you as an alarm clock to let you know when it's time to reach out a helping hand. Don't hit the snooze button. Ask God when and how to help.

~ ~ ~

The Christian's compassion must be like God's—unceasing.

WILLIAM BARCLAY

When you make that one effort to feel
compassion instead of blame or self-blame,
the heart opens again and continues opening.

SARA PADDISON

I would rather make mistakes in kindness
and compassion than work miracles
in unkindness and hardness.

MOTHER TERESA

By compassion we make others' misery our own,
and so, by relieving them,
we relieve ourselves also.

SIR THOMAS BROWNE

Be kind and compassionate to one another,
forgiving each other,
just as in Christ God forgave you.

EPHESIANS 4:32 NIV

God is so good, and by raising Jesus from death,
he has given us new life and a hope that lives on.

1 PETER 1:3 CEV

There are no hopeless causes when you are moving in the direction God has asked you to go. Circumstances may look hopeless, when viewed from an earthly perspective. But from God's point of view, victory for every one of His children—and that includes you—is certain.

When life feels overwhelming and what you've hoped for seems out of reach, ask God to help you see things from His point of view. Meditate on what you know to be true: God is good. His promises never fail. Your destiny is secure. Nothing can separate you from His love.

When all seems lost, hold on to what you know you've found. Let the hope of what you know to be true carry you through.

Do not look to your hope, but to Christ, the source of your hope.

CHARLES HADDON SPURGEON

Hope is the physician of every misery.

IRISH PROVERB

What oxygen is to the lungs,
such is hope for the meaning of life.

HEINRICH EMIL BRUNNER

There is no medicine like hope, no incentive
so great, and no tonic so powerful as expectation
of something tomorrow.

SAMUEL JOHNSON

*May the God of hope fill you with all joy and peace
as you trust in him, so that you may overflow with
hope by the power of the Holy Spirit.*

ROMANS 15:13 NIV

Patience

God will strengthen you with his own great power.
And you will not give up when troubles come,
but you will be patient.

COLOSSIANS 1:11 ICB

It's annoying to be kept waiting. It makes you feel as though the one you're waiting for doesn't value your time, as though that person is in control—and you're not.

That's why waiting on God is so good for you. It's a subtle reminder you're not in charge of the universe. If God answered your prayers exactly the way you thought best in the time frame that was most to your liking, after a while you'd begin to believe life really was all about you.

As God builds patience into your life, He also uses those around you to help it grow. Motherhood is an especially fertile testing ground. Who knows what opportunities for growth you'll be given today?

Teach us, O Lord, the disciplines of patience,
for to wait is often harder than to work.

PETER MARSHALL

Be patient toward all that is unsolved
in your heart.

DAG HAMMARSKJÖLD

Be patient with everyone, but above all,
with yourself.

SAINT FRANCIS DE SALES

Patience is bitter, but its fruit is sweet.

JEAN-JACQUES ROUSSEAU

Be patient when trouble comes.
Pray at all times.

ROMANS 12:12 ICB

Heaven

*He puts a little of heaven in our hearts
so that we'll never settle for less.*

2 CORINTHIANS 5:5 THE MESSAGE

*L*ook around your home. It's real. You can touch the walls, turn on the lights, and relax in your own bed. It holds both memories and expectations. It's a place where love is free to grow.

Heaven is just as real. Although it isn't time for you to experience it yet, the Bible offers you a small taste of what your future home will be like. It says it will be a place of eternal beauty, where tears will no longer fall. It also says God's preparing a place there just for you.

The evening news is a daily reminder you're not home yet. Instead of letting that fact discourage you, let it fill your heart with the sweet anticipation of what lies ahead.

Earth has no sorrow that heaven cannot heal.

THOMAS V. MOORE

Heaven will be the perfection we have always longed for. All the things that made earth unlovely and tragic will be absent in heaven.

BILLY GRAHAM

Heaven is a prepared place for a prepared people.

LEWIS SPERRY CHAFER

God's retirement plan is out of this world.

AUTHOR UNKNOWN

We know that our body—the tent we live in here on earth—will be destroyed. But when that happens, God will have a house for us to live in. It will not be a house made by men. It will be a home in heaven that will last forever.

2 CORINTHIANS 5:1 ICB

Letting Go

*There's an opportune time to do things,
a right time for everything on the earth: ...
A right time to hold on and another to let go.*

ECCLESIASTES 3:1, 6 THE MESSAGE

Letting go of anything that is precious to you is difficult. Letting go of your children is perhaps the most difficult of all. But as they reach adulthood, your children need to let go of your hand, so they can take a tighter grip on God's.

Even now, your grasp should be loosening. You need to give your children the freedom to become who God created them to be—which may look a bit different from the people you imagined they'd become.

Though the influence of your physical presence will lessen as time goes by, the power of your prayers need not. As you hold your children tightly in prayer, you can trust God's nurturing love to guide them with tender parental care.

Trust involves letting go and knowing
God will catch you.

JAMES C. DOBSON

I have held many things in my hands,
and I have lost them all; but whatever
I have placed in God's hands, that I still possess.

CORRIE TEN BOOM

The weakest saint can experience the power
of the deity of the Son of God
if he is willing to let go.

OSWALD CHAMBERS

Treasures in heaven are laid up only
as treasures on earth are laid down.

AUTHOR UNKNOWN

*Jesus said, "If you try to keep your life for yourself,
you will lose it. But if you give up your life for my sake
and for the sake of the Good News,
you will find true life."*

MARK 8:35 NLT

Scripture

Let the words of Christ, in all their richness,
live in your hearts and make you wise.

COLOSSIANS 3:16 NLT

Imagine you're cleaning the kitchen. All of a sudden you hear the voice of God speaking directly to you. What do you do? Ask Him to come back when the chores are done? Pretend like your listening, but really concentrate on getting that spaghetti stain off the counter? No, you drop whatever you're doing, fall to your knees, and hang on every word He says.

The truth is, God's voice is speaking—every minute of every day. To hear it, all you need to do is open your Bible. God speaks about relationships, eternal truth, and the future. He also provides encouragement, guidance, comfort, even guidelines on how to be a better parent.

God's Word has the power to change your life. Are you listening?

When you have read the Bible, you will know
it is the word of God, because you will have
found it the key to your own heart,
your own happiness and your duty.

WOODROW WILSON

The Bible is God's chart for you to steer by,
to keep you from the bottom of the sea,
and to show you where the harbor is, and how
to reach it without running on rocks and bars.

HENRY WARD BEECHER

When you read God's word you must constantly
be saying to yourself, "It is talking to me,
and about me."

SØREN KIERKEGAARD

God did not write a book and send it
by messenger to be read at a distance by unaided
minds. He spoke a Book and lives in His spoken
words, constantly speaking His words and causing
the power of them to persist across the years.

A. W. TOZER

Using the Scriptures, the person who serves God
will be ready and will have everything
he needs to do every good work.

2 TIMOTHY 3:17 ICB

*Because of [Christ] all the parts of the body
care for each other and help each other.*

COLOSSIANS 2:19 ICB

It's obvious kids need help. That's one of your jobs as a mom, to help your kids learn to walk, talk, tie their shoes, drive a car, maybe even learn to speak Chinese. But moms need help too. It's a need people never outgrow.

God designed you to live in relationship with Him and other people. Part of being in relationship is supporting those you love when their hands are full, their bodies are weary, or their hearts are heavy.

Accepting help from others is just as important as reaching out to help them. So, don't suffer in silence. Ask for help from your husband, your friends, your kids, and especially God. It can mean the difference between success and meltdown.

Light is the task where many share the toil.

HOMER

God has so ordered that men, being in need
of each other, should learn to love each other,
and bear each other's burdens.

GEORGE AUGUSTUS SALA

There are friends who sail together
Through quiet waters and stormy weather
Helping each other through joy and through strife.
And they are the kind who give meaning to life.

AUTHOR UNKNOWN

A friend is never known until a man have need.

JOHN HEYWOOD

By helping each other with your troubles,
you truly obey the law of Christ.

GALATIANS 6:2 NCV

Growth

Let the wonderful kindness and the understanding
that come from our Lord and Savior Jesus Christ
help you to keep on growing.

2 PETER 3:18 CEV

*B*aby books record every step of a child's
growth. When we become adults, we
don't stop growing. Unfortunately, we often stop
celebrating those milestones we pass along the road
toward maturity.

Maturity isn't a stage of life. It's a lifelong
process. So, why not celebrate your progress? Ask
God to help you see where you've grown, as well
as what areas of your life could use a little extra
attention. Perhaps you've made great strides in the
anger department, but your habit of dealing with
discouragement by heading to the mall to make a
little "pick-me-up" purchase is still a struggle. Like
any proud Parent, God is celebrating the good while
encouraging you toward further growth. Take time
out to do the same.

If we don't change, we don't grow. If we don't
grow, we are not really living. Growth demands
a temporary surrender of security.

GAIL SHEEHY

Gradual growth in grace, knowledge, faith, love,
holiness, humility, and spiritual-mindedness—
all this I see clearly taught and urged in Scripture.
But sudden, instantaneous leaps from conversion
to consecration, I fail to see in the Bible.

J. C. RYLE

Progress in the Christian life is exactly equal
to the growing knowledge we gain of
the Triune God in personal experience.

A. W. TOZER

Be not afraid of growing slowly;
be afraid only of standing still.

CHINESE PROVERB

We must grow up in every way into him
who is the head, into Christ.

EPHESIANS 4:15 NRSV

Integrity

Whoever walks in integrity walks securely.

PROVERBS 10:9 NRSV

*Y*our integrity is a gift to God, your children, and yourself. It's a sign you're willing to do what God asks, no matter what others say. It lets those around you know you can be trusted to do the right thing for all the right reasons. A woman of integrity is a mom who can be proud to have her children walk in her footsteps.

Today's culture doesn't hold integrity in the same high esteem. Commitment, honesty, truth, and morality are all relative. Their definitions can change, depending on the circumstances that surround them.

God and His truth never change, however. Walking in ways that please Him is not only wise, but also makes life easier for you and your family.

Integrity is not a conditional word.
It doesn't blow in the wind or change
with the weather.

JOHN D. MACDONALD

Integrity is the noblest possession.

LATIN PROVERB

There is no such thing as a minor lapse
of integrity.

TOM PETERS

Integrity has no need of rules.

ALBERT CAMUS

Let integrity and uprightness preserve me,
for I wait for You.

PSALM 25:21

Gentleness

Your gentleness has made me great.

Gentleness is not the opposite of strength. It's what gives true strength compassionate power. In the same way a gentle touch and quiet words will calm a crying child more effectively than a harsh rebuke, a gentle spirit will enable you to be more approachable, and effectual, in the lives of others.

God is the master carpenter when it comes to rounding off harsh edges in your character. Ask Him to make you more like Jesus. Jesus treated others with confident honesty, tempered by gentle respect. That's because He deeply loved everyone He met.

The more your love for others grows, the more precious they will become to you and the more gently you will desire to treat them.

~ ~ ~

Power can do by gentleness what
violence fails to accomplish.

Feelings are everywhere ... be gentle.

J. MASAI

Instead of losing, the gentle gain.
Instead of being ripped off and
taken advantage of, they come out ahead!

CHARLES R. SWINDOLL

Nothing is so strong as gentleness,
nothing so gentle as real strength.

SAINT FRANCIS DE SALES

Let your gentleness be known to everyone.

PHILIPPIANS 4:5 NRSV

Trust

Trust in the LORD, and do good.

PSALM 37:3

*T*rust encourages growth. The more you trust your children's judgment, the more freedom you'll give them, and the more they'll have the chance to mature. The more you trust God's love, the more you'll act on what He asks you to do, thereby giving your faith a greater opportunity to grow.

But trust goes deeper than words. You can't just tell your kids you trust they're safe drivers. You have to go a step further. You have to hand them the keys to the car.

Moving forward in faith can be scary at times, but the more you put trust to the test—and the one you trust is proven faithful—the easier it becomes. In what area do you need to trust God today?

Trust in God and you are never to be confounded in time or in eternity.

DWIGHT MOODY

Trust the past to God's mercy, the present
to God's love and the future to God's providence.

SAINT AUGUSTINE OF HIPPO

The highest pinnacle of the spiritual life is not
happy joy in unbroken sunshine, but absolute
and undoubting trust in the love of God.

A. W. THOROLD

All I have seen teaches me to trust
the Creator for all I have not seen.

RALPH WALDO EMERSON

Trust in him at all times, O people;
pour out your heart before him;
God is a refuge for us.

PSALM 62:8 NRSV

*Warn the rich people of this world not to be proud
or to trust in wealth that is easily lost.*

1 TIMOTHY 6:17 CEV

*A*s a mother, you've been given great wealth. You've been entrusted with the priceless gift of a child. There's nothing you could acquire from a catalog or eBay® that could ever come close to the worth of raising a family.

But how tempting those other trinkets seem to be. The more they take up of your heart, the more they will take up of your home, your time, and your life. When the desire to acquire strikes, take a moment to focus on the riches that already surround you, treasure that can never be lost or stolen, that will last throughout eternity.

～ ～ ～

The real measure of our wealth is how much
we'd be worth if we lost all our money.

JOHN HENRY JOWETT

If you want to feel rich, just count all the things
you have that money can't buy.

AUTHOR UNKNOWN

There is nothing wrong with people
possessing riches. The wrong comes when
riches possess people.

BILLY GRAHAM

God only, not wealth, maintains the world.

MARTIN LUTHER

*Better the little that the righteous have than
the wealth of many wicked.*

PSALM 37:16 NIV

Protection

You are a hiding place for me;
you preserve me from trouble.

PSALM 32:7 NRSV

At one time or another, every mother prays for her children's safety—even those mothers who may not realize God is listening. An illness, a driver's permit, even a class bully can stir a mother's heart to cry out for protection for the ones she loves.

Yet, some of these prayers seem to go unheard, or at least unanswered. The reality is that God is there, cradling you and your children in His arms when danger is near. Sometimes, He offers aid through miraculous circumstances. Sometimes, He allows natural consequences to take place, even to the innocent. But that doesn't mean His love has run dry. God's protection reaches beyond this world into eternity. You can trust Him with what is most precious to you.

~ ~ ~

Those who walk in God's shadow
are not shaken by the storm.

ANDREA GARNEY

Prayer is the key that shuts us up
under his protection and safeguard.

JACQUES ELLUL

Safe am I. Safe am I, in the hollow of His hand.

OLD SUNDAY SCHOOL SONG

Security is not the absence of danger,
but the presence of God,
no matter what the danger.

AUTHOR UNKNOWN

The LORD will keep you from all evil;
he will keep your life. The LORD will keep
your going out and your coming in from
this time on and forevermore.

PSALM 121:7–8 NRSV

Generosity

*Jesus said, "Live generously and graciously
toward others, the way God lives toward you."*
MATTHEW 5:48 THE MESSAGE

It's easy to be generous with a double batch of chocolate chip cookies. But when it gets down to the last one, generosity becomes a bit more of a challenge. The same is true with every area of your life, including your time, your money, and your possessions.

However, true generosity always costs something. It doesn't give out of excess, the desire for praise, or even guilt. Generosity gives because it sees a need—and love longs to fill it.

Everything you have to share with others is only yours because of God's generosity to you. It gave Him pleasure to give you those gifts. Discover the pleasure of giving to others by following God's example.

He who gives what he would as readily
throw away, gives without generosity;
for the essence of generosity is in self-sacrifice.
SIR HENRY TAYLOR

Life begets life. Energy begets energy.
It is by spending oneself that
one becomes rich.

SARAH BERNHARDT

Giving is a joy if we do it in the right spirit.
It all depends on whether we think of it as
"What can I spare?" or as "What can I share?"

ESTHER YORK BURKHOLDER

You do not have to be rich to be generous.
If he has the spirit of true generosity,
a pauper can give like a prince.

CORRINE U. WELLS

A generous person will be enriched.

PROVERBS 11:25 NRSV

God's Love

*The Lord said, "I have loved you
with an everlasting love; therefore
with lovingkindness I have drawn you.*

JEREMIAH 31:3

*C*reation is a love story. God's love is so all-encompassing He had to create beings to lavish it on. When He made the human heart, He designed it to crave what He longed to give.

This longing for love is alive in you and your children today. Your own imperfect love can't fill that hunger in your children's hearts, just as their love for you will never fully satisfy your own heart. Only God invites you into a love story where you can be wholly satisfied and eternally cherished—where you can be complete.

Welcome God, and His love, into your life with open arms. With Him, "happily ever after" is not a fairy tale, but a promise.

~ ~ ~

Every existing thing is equally upheld
in its existence by God's creative love.

SIMONE WEIL

God does not love us because we are valuable.
We are valuable because God loves us.

FULTON JOHN SHEEN

God soon turns from his wrath,
but he never turns from his love.

CHARLES HADDON SPURGEON

The person you are now, the person
you have been, the person you will be—
this person God has chosen as beloved.

WILLIAM COUNTRYMAN

I am persuaded that neither death nor life,
nor angels nor principalities nor powers, nor things
present nor things to come, nor height nor depth,
nor any other created thing, shall be able to
separate us from the love of God.

ROMANS 8:38–39

Our only goal is to please God.

2 CORINTHIANS 5:9 ICB

*C*onsider your goals in life. They may include things like being a good mom, getting a college degree, or writing a mystery novel. Goals are as individual as the people who strive to achieve them.

They are also important. Having a goal challenges you to reach beyond where you are right now. It helps direct how you spend your time, energy, and resources. Even seemingly insignificant goals help influence the course of your life.

Are your personal goals worthy of the attention you're giving them? Examine the motivations behind them. If these motivations would please God, then the goal is worth pursuing with enthusiasm and excellence.

First build a proper goal. That proper goal
will make it easy, almost automatic,
to build a proper you.

JOHANN WOLFGANG VON GOETHE

The goal of a virtuous life is to become like God.

GREGORY OF NYSSA

You become successful the moment
you start moving toward a worthwhile goal.

AUTHOR UNKNOWN

The tragedy in life doesn't lie in not
reaching your goal. The tragedy lies in
having no goal to reach.

BENJAMIN MAYS

Forgetting what lies behind and straining forward
to what lies ahead, I press on toward the goal for
the prize of the heavenly call of God in Christ Jesus.

PHILIPPIANS 3:13–14 NRSV

The LORD will be your confidence.

PROVERBS 3:26 NIV

*B*eing self-confident is a good thing. Being God-confident is even better. It's fine to believe in yourself and your abilities, to be able to tackle what comes your way with self-assurance. But only by being confident in who God is and who He says you are, will you have a realistic picture of what you're really capable of.

Take confidence in this: God is all-powerful, infinitely wise, and eternally loving—He's on your side. God is guiding you toward maturity and victory every day of your life. He has created you with unique gifts and talents that will bring you delight when you put them to use.

Step out in God-confidence. God's love, power, and forgiveness allow you to hold your head high.

I place no hope in my strength, nor in my works, but all my confidence is in God.

FRANÇOIS RABELAIS

Nothing can be done without hope
and confidence.

HELEN KELLER

The greater and more persistent your confidence
in God, the more abundantly you
will receive all that you ask.

ALBERT THE GREAT

Confidence in the natural world is self-reliance,
in the spiritual world it is God-reliance.

OSWALD CHAMBERS

In quietness and confidence shall be your strength.

ISAIAH 30:15

Work

Commit your work to the LORD,
and your plans will be established.

PROVERBS 16:3 NRSV

*I*t's been said motherhood is the toughest job in the world. That's a hard point to argue. Sure, the benefits are great. But you're on call twenty-four hours a day with a job description that includes qualifications for nurse, teacher, housekeeper, activity director, nutritionist, disciplinarian, and counselor—to name just a few.

Even the smallest of your responsibilities can have a big impact on the lives of your kids. You need the stamina of a pack mule and the wisdom of … well, God.

Commit every aspect of this vital job to Him. Let your love for God, as well as for your kids, inspire you to humbly and attentively put your whole heart into every task you find before you.

Hard work is a thrill and joy when
you are in the will of God.

ROBERT A. COOK

Work is not a curse, it is a blessing from God.

JOHN PAUL II

Honest labor bears a lovely face.

THOMAS DEKKER

He who labors as he prays lifts up his heart
to God with his hands.

SAINT BERNARD OF CLAIRVAUX

In all the work you are doing, work the best you can.
Work as if you were working for the Lord,
not for men.

COLOSSIANS 3:23 ICB

Life

Jesus said, "I came so they can have real
and eternal life, more and better life
than they ever dreamed of."

JOHN 10:10 THE MESSAGE

Life is lived one moment at a time. Making each moment count in a way that adds up to a life well lived takes decisiveness and perseverance. It's easy to simply go through the motions of an ordinary day because they feel so familiar—run the carpool, feed the family, head to the grocery store, fall into bed exhausted. But consider the fact that every encounter you have with another person is a chance for God's glory to shine through you. Every task you undertake is an opportunity for excellence and personal growth.

Ordinary days have the potential to become extraordinary. Rediscover simple pleasures. Let your words enrich those around you. Love deeply. Draw closer to God continually. Live this moment fully awake and alive.

I will not just live my life.
I will not just spend my life. I will invest my life.

HELEN KELLER

Life is a great big canvas;
throw all the paint on it you can.

DANNY KAYE

Let God have your life;
he can do more with it than you can.

DWIGHT MOODY

The value of life lies not in the length of days,
but in the use we make of them.

MICHEL DE MONTAIGNE

The way you tell me to live is always right;
help me understand it so I can live to the fullest.

PSALM 119:144 THE MESSAGE

God's Faithfulness

Hear my prayer, O Lord; answer my plea
because you are faithful to your promises.

PSALM 143:1 TLB

"*Never*" and "*always*" are two words that are tough to use without exaggerating—or tempering with an exception or two. But with God, "*never*" and "*always*" can be used accurately and often: God is always near. God's love will never fail. God always keeps His promises. God's generosity never ends.

These statements are true because God is faithful. His character doesn't change. That means what was true about God two thousand years ago is true today and will be true tomorrow. There are no exceptions.

God's absolute faithfulness is a solid foundation for risk-taking faith. You can dare to depend on what God says, because you know He won't change His mind. You can always trust God's faithfulness will never fail.

~ ~ ~

God is faithful, and if we serve him faithfully,
he will provide for our needs.

SAINT RICHARD OF CHICHESTER

What more powerful consideration can be
thought on to make us true to God,
than the faithfulness and truth of God to us?

WILLIAM GURNALL

In God's faithfulness lies eternal security.

CORRIE TEN BOOM

Though men are false, God is faithful.

MATTHEW HENRY

*God is faithful; by him you were called into
the fellowship of his Son, Jesus Christ our Lord.*

1 CORINTHIANS 1:9 NRSV

Contentment

Serving God makes us very rich,
if we are satisfied with what we have.

1 Timothy 6:6 ncv

*L*ook in the mirror. Look at the décor of your home. Look at the balance in your checkbook. Look at the responsibilities motherhood has set before you today. Now, ask yourself honestly, Am I content?

Allow God to show you any areas in your life where you're hungry for more. Then, ask Him to reveal what lies beneath the surface of that ache of discontent. Perhaps pride, greed, or a longing for the acceptance of others is preventing you from finding true satisfaction in what God has given you. Whatever it is, tell God about it. Ask Him for forgiveness, as well as a change of heart. Let God show you how to celebrate where you are right now.

God is most glorified in us when we are most satisfied in him.

John Piper

The secret of contentment is the realization
that life is a gift, not a right.

AUTHOR UNKNOWN

The utmost we can hope for in this life
is contentment.

JOSEPH ADDISON

A little is as much as a lot, if it is enough.

STEVE BROWN

I have learned to be content with whatever I have.

PHILIPPIANS 4:11 NRSV

Jesus said, "Love the Lord God with all your passion
and prayer and intelligence and energy."

MARK 12:30 THE MESSAGE

here is no greater motivator in life than love. It's what gets you out of bed for a three o'clock feeding. It's what leads you to sacrifice your time for a total stranger. It's what draws you toward God. It's what held Jesus on the cross.

Love may be an emotion, but love isn't sincere until that emotion has inspired selfless action. Love never runs out of reasons to give.

Pay attention to what love leads you to do today—your love for God, for your children, your spouse, your friends, perhaps even for a stranger at the deli counter. Don't hold back. Put your love into action.

Love is the thing that makes life possible or, indeed, tolerable.

ARNOLD JOSEPH TOYNBEE

I have found the paradox that if I love until
it hurts, then there is no hurt, but only more love.

MOTHER TERESA

Love seeks one thing only:
the good of the one loved.

THOMAS MERTON

Love, like warmth, should beam forth
on every side and bend to every necessity
of our brethren.

MARTIN LUTHER

Beloved, let us love one another, for love is from God;
and everyone who loves is born of God
and knows God.

1 JOHN 4:7 NASB

Seasons of Life

I will be your God through all you lifetime,
yes, even when your hair is white with age.

ISAIAH 46:4 TLB

*E*very season has its challenges and
beauty ... the joy of building a snowman
and the trial of getting your car safely across a patch
of black ice, the relaxation of lying on the beach and
the pain of an unexpected sunburn.

Like every season of life, motherhood is a mixed
blessing. There are warmhearted hugs and sleepless
nights, treasured words and time-outs, sweet victories
and bitter disappointments.

Seasons change. Before you know it, you'll be
looking back on where you are right now. Chances
are, what you'll remember most are the good times.
Don't wait until tomorrow to appreciate today. Grab
hold of the transient joys this season brings your way.
Celebrate the blessings. Pull together during the hard
times. Thank God for each day.

Gratitude is a seasoning for all seasons.

AUTHOR UNKNOWN

I have lived,
And seen God's hand thro a lifetime,
And all was for best.

ROBERT BROWNING

Every day should be passed as if
it were to be our last.

PUBLILIUS SYRUS

Every moment of this strange and lovely life from
dawn to dusk is a miracle. Somewhere, always,
a rose is opening its petals to the dawn.
Somewhere, always, a flower is fading in the dusk.

BEVERLEY NICHOLS

They delight in doing everything the LORD wants;
day and night they think about his law.
They are like trees planted along the riverbank,
bearing fruit each season without fail.

PSALM 1:2–3 NLT

Topical Index

Additional copies of this book and other titles
from ELM HILL PRESS are available from
your local bookstore.

Other titles in this series:

God's Daily Answer
God's Daily Answer Devotional
God's Daily Answer for Women
God's Daily Answer for Men
God's Daily Answer for Grads
God's Daily Answer for Teachers